I0178238

TRUE DOES NOTHING

J.T. Barbarese

a plume editions book

AN IMPRINT OF MADHAT PRESS

ASHEVILLE, NORTH CAROLINA

MadHat Press
MadHat Incorporated
PO Box 8364, Asheville, NC 28814

Copyright © 2018 J.T. Barbarese
All rights reserved

The Library of Congress has assigned
this edition a Control Number of
2018931199

ISBN 978-1-941196-65-6 (paperback)

Text by J.T. Barbarese
Cover image by Marc Vincenz
Cover design by Marc Vincenz

Plume Editions
an imprint of MadHat Press
www.MadHat-Press.com

First Printing

Table of Contents

True does nothing, successfully. False does nothing, unsuccessfully.

—The Unix System User's Manual

Please Stand If You Are Able

So long since we all had extended meanings, head colds in April,
    thunder at Christmas, yonic moons in October, walking all
    over.
Degrees from the University of No-Strings, parading in black
    nostalgias and blobby gowns, we lobbed caps over pickets,
bobbed like puppets in camo,
shot up slopes, came home, shot up for real,
ate the black cheese of defeat, drank the painful waters,
could not eat the bread we made.

For Bible Study, Corinthians 1:13, Gospel Lesson, Matthew 5:1-6,
for Tithes and Offerings sing *Jesu, Jesu,*
the Children's Message is elephant pockets, the Sermon a man
    in a grease suit, Communion, intinction, and Fellowship
    breakfast is canceled.

Please stand if you are able for the Lord's Prayer.

The Doxology is a praise song
for those who play chicken with tanks,
for those who did not go looking and those who did,
for the girl on the levee holding a doll so tight I had to turn down
    the sound,
for the leafleted tossing the leaflet back at the leafleters,

and Benediction will be silent, sullen, and quick.
May you get out and get home safely,
and hold your palm to a wall, any wall, and feel no fire.

J. T. Barbarese

Old Ratty Bush by the Seawall in Cape May

If to come here is to think eternity, or maybe not think, but feel
      with precision,
if I am meant to come all this way,
and I don't mean just to Cape May,
it is to see this, which is not a *this,* so I call it *you,* or *Thou,*
    and your exacting greenness
hanging rat-branched over squatness, you too a squatter, you make
      me forget what I was going to say,
bursting from left-overs, rubbishy concrete from some razed
      chamber of commerce or shut down movie theater, fed on
      native sand, feeding the dunes and debris,

so, then, you are enough, you are enough,
so is this sand (sand is not a thee or a thou) islanding the chunked
      concrete and bushes as brown as the faces of shrimpers that
      time in New Orleans,
(bad Country and Western is pouring from the miniature golf course,
      and you, stiff and silent, face it like a baffled neighbor)
isn't that enough, aren't you enough for me?
I usually avoid poems like this, about dumps, dumpsters, trashcans,
      weedy life and weedy lives, it comes more naturally to Jerry,
the drivel describing how you have an experience of yourself that
      instantly renders the rest of life incomplete, your whole past
      an archaic torso of [fill in the blanks]
but not this afternoon,
because you foreground a holy emptiness that would, if we were not
      broken, make us walk into the waves like V.W., her body
      found three weeks later against Southease Bridge,
because that's your fate, to be a snot-green rag of a bush wrapped
      around more of you that is becoming less and less, blocking
      the view,

to live on the down-low in front of all this gay blue waste, these
       deadpan clouds smiling emptily over water, these gulls
       (silenced from here by the C&W) like paste-on eyebrows,

framing us, an umbrella'd herd, cabana'd, capped and mohawked
       with our volleyballs and poised Frisbees and retro jerseys,
       dragged by speedboats, holding balloons, our bodies washed
       up against bridges, bridges washed up against shores,

O unvanquished and unyielding you, and you're not much,
compared to this vast blue that to us is nothing, to thee or to me, so
       against thee I fling my body, my voice, all that I am

Calvin's God

The old woman dragging
the quilt up 7th Ave,
the tire-changer leaning against the plug,

the woman with an ashen brow
in a sudden shower,
the ashes running into her mascara,

the girl to my left
sobbing,
picking out cards

Aunt May telling Uncle John
Arbeit macht frei
but not where she has been all day,

the torrid-faced diner
whose bald head
has burned up the sunlight,

and the dry drunk
who doesn't believe in accidents
and ends up president.

On a Sentence from Benjamin

Warmth is ebbing from things.

Days like this, I miss you,
a few classy hankies of storm trailing the sun,
glare-bursts on goose-water,
the groundhogs like loaves of challah on the grass on the traffic
    islands,
cars with children at the windows at the idling light.

I miss the sublime average, I miss mediocrity, life before metal
    revelations and engirdled heights, before uptalk and wifi,
I miss the unmixed blessing of just what's here, uncollected pocket
    litter, the stray packets of oyster crackers, the fenced yards,
    the R-8 shaking the fence, the wind spinning the tire swing,
shaving's sleepy arousals, the pleasure of steamed glass, and
    showering in back of the shed under the caterpillar cocoons,
    hung from your peach tree like living cotton candy

I miss the security of dullness and how it stops the everyday from
    hurting itself,
pedestrians wrapped in sunglare, teens making out in public, the
    blurry tattoos and piercings, the third eye on an eyelid, the
    bright grim first June heat-wave,
how mown grass can smell like crotch, how the splinted make-out
    benches with old carved hieroglyphs are national treasures,
heart-and-arrow haikus on trees and delts,
how the pissed-on seats on the Riverline smell almost like fresh
    coffee, O

the average peripheries, the average visions, which are the walls of
    our prism, the
blessed typical, the take or leave it look of rain racing down the
    trolley tracks on Germantown Avenue,
the narrow beam of light on the wall, descending as the sun lifts over
    the house.

All That Fullness

and there are details,
>   the conjoined backyards, the fences smiling across the
>   decades of kudzu trucked from the Carolinas, o
>   disastrous import,
>   the dignified vegetal slump into the railroad bank as if this is
>   the promised end, o what gravitas,
>   the cars in repose by the curb, even the trashcans with their
>   hard open mouths singing Hey Bob-a-Rebop to the
>   flies,
>   the century sycamores risen forty feet higher than the
>   houses, debarking or barkless and rocking the ravens
>   and starlings,
>   the slug slime on hollyhocks, the concert of dozens of mass-
>   produced wind chimes tinkling from open porches,
>   neighbor Paul with his apnea machine, his wife with her
>   bad foot, front lawns overrun with narcissi, flattened
>   condoms among the clippings,
>   this should be enough, for anyone, especially such as you
>   after your infidelities, rages, breaks, hypnagogic past
>   noon,
>   but none of it is,
>   not her fullness so mixed in your life-junk, a commingling
>   of flesh and furniture, fur and flesh,
>   her small Biblical hands and arms browned on the back of
>   the clawed chair where the cats slept, her desperate
>   housepets,
>   why isn't this enough,
>   isn't Halloween enough, a convenience store you can walk to
>   at midnight, Town Watch and a stickered car, a Shop
>   Vac and painted house numbers,

what price satisfaction if you can't walk to a store without
     your wallet, and who are you to dismiss the winter
     humming in the overheads
and spring plucking the legacy antennas like wild kabuki on
     the roofs talking Urdu to the west winds
and the May blizzards of cottonwood spore, and the linden
     snow yellowing fenders and windshields of cars you
     can leave unlocked all day?

With such decency the cyclone fence bends and is bent, with
     what nobility the man-made collapses into Spinozist
     eternity,
so who are you to walk off, leave her and the house barren,
     and leave them in front of monitors writing *All those
     years* and *if only if only*
then dream of her cradling a watch the size of a Maine
     Coon, sobbing and pointing to six p.m. under a
     lowering sky?
O, look out of that rear window now onto the backyards,
     dream-conjoined, contiguous, fenceless, fantastic,
     extensive, gone.

Close Out

for Niccolo

In the parking lot the young bulls wax cars, all green synthetic mesh
      and identical Iverson jerseys,
and in long cool Caddies parked in the shade, the shiny and un-
      sweating elders with quintuple bypasses, engines running,
      a-c churning, looking on
eyeing their wives or their babes or somebody's else's wife or babe
      disappearing through the electronic eye, pushing carts.

I am overwhelmed here, by America's products, I feel nothing,
so I bend and smell your hair, kiss it and taste your compounding
      mettle
—salt, the sour sweetness of sweat and breast milk,
and some third thing, faintly ureic,
sweet, fecal, and elemental—

and I am back in my body, I am back from commercial,
the war in the Mideast is over, the collapse is reversed, the Wild
      Weasels gone back to Fort Dix, F-10s unscrambled, the body
      bags back in storage,
and I am not in the middle of Bradlees', I am awake now,
a man holding his infant son, loading a cart, convinced
that Velcro and Spandex are signs of the Apocalypse,

even earlier than myself, than you, than Velcro,
I am in the earliest place,
I am alone in the night of origins, and it is just me and you, my love,
      tasting our swampy beginnings.

J. T. Barbarese

Epitaph

for Ralph Allen (1942–2005)

Lived in the suburbs of the century,
    the beer-stink pool halls of blunts and crackpots with plans,
in basements with mimeographs and newsletters,
leafleting corners where he talked to cops and counter-leafletters,
bought them lunch,
worked corners talking politics, parking lots where people scored
        junk,
worked snake-hung woods where wobbly geese shat green and
        hissed,
worked beyond the mile-markers, talked to undercover spooks who
    talked to their shoulders and snapped the fog, covered in peace
    buttons,

biked to his job at Germantown Academy every day, a 14-mile
        round trip,
taught middle school thirty years, married forty to one woman,
understood fruit trees, had a dog named Aria and would talk to her
    some nights when the moon was full,

hiked Appalachia, rode with the Freedom Riders, Mississippi '60s,
    lost with Stevenson, King, Kennedy, McCarthy, heartbroken
        over McGovern,
understated in rare victory, ever generous in defeat,
    wrote poems and never typed them, loved "shaping the letters,"

hooked church with his older brother and spent the tithe on ice
    cream.

Shut Up

Ernest, reading Matthew 11:6, aloud, fearful you'll be lost, so
        agitated you're unable to read silently,
a man your age wearing earbuds a table over is running spreadsheets,
        the girl across from him is studying the voiceless molecules
        that make up air
and putting on makeup in her computer screen, and I am here with
        a beautiful woman and listening to you instead of to her, so
        do shut up,

all we can do is stand in the middle of all that is done and endure it,
        beginning to end, unlorded, unsponsored, unmastered and
        -mistressed,
there are no angels in the fridge, there are no demons in the tacos,
        Michelangelo's
putti were based on actual adolescent streetrats, and half the
        madonnas were *putane,* who worked for lunch money and
        carfare,
and since God is not even in the details, be quiet, Ernest, and listen

the plants whistle up to the sun, the sun yells down to the apples
        and plums till they turn Punic purple in rage
and they swell because they're awake now, and will not be silent

Independence Day

As the old woman from Belarus said to her granddaughter,
    You will never know what it was like,
and maybe you shouldn't—Gramma said,
remembering all the dead,
counting to twenty million on ten fingers and two claws,
sighting down the single thought that survived her.
It's the thought she left her granddaughter,
a smart blonde who finally got her degree,
entered the global economy
in an A-line dress
and a Buster Brown haircut.
I think of her
and see her grandmother,
blown up Ukrainian zoos and empty cages,
craters filling with snow,
    no dog safe from the stewpot,
young women waiting
for nothing to wait for
empty trains pulling in, pulling out. We know
nothing and maybe we shouldn't. Overhead,
another fake airburst, carnival colors,
unreal bombs,
ecstatic drunks on the balconies,
    cop stops every corner.

Boy Slapped, Sobbing to Catch His Breath

One good slap. Then nothing,
just wind rattling empty Sprite cans,
SUV's crunching gravel,

and Billy's mom
in a tee-shirt with
I'm Billy's Mother

in Phillies red
slamming one door, two,
gunning the engine, gone.

O Lord,
deliver us from the rest of us
now and at the hour

we miss the cut-off,
the take sign, the steal sign,
the very ball,

now and at the hour
we call on Thee, O Lord,
and instead get Billy's mother.

No Selfies for Mary

In the mausoleum shadow, eye-mopping mother, O Mary,
married to the carpenter, living in alienation in an unfurnished
      studio, cable wheels for chairs, wine crates for bookshelves,
      bare floors and tools underfoot,
no fun, this life, kid-encumbered, and now kid-less and solo,
no husband around when your only child is executed, guess he's too
      busy, at least he never appears in the Stations or on the holy
      cards,
O full of grace and all-loving and loving what never loved back,
for his love was a cloth thrown over a spill, his love was a climate,
      global, not local, tell me

whose Kleenex, Mary, whose tissues, whose bright black pumps,
whose missal, whose limo, whose purse, whose dress, whose
      compact,
whose mother when you become that Other, The Virgin Mother,
whose borrowed black death suit, who will clean the suit?

Turning from the phone-pointers, relatives fanning themselves with
      mass cards, tears on the pants suits and pinstripes, stale
      breath, stale aromatics,
funeral director hand-rubbing and quickly approaching, handing
      out maps to Holy Cross,
relatives queuing for the final rose-chuck, four pall bearers, two
      cousins, two strangers, in suits lifting shovels, a fist of earth
      on each shiny tongue,
drivers whispering *Where are his* [expletive] *friends,* smell of diesel
      and honeysuckle, sexual odor of newly turned earth, rank
      and rained-on,
somebody's nephew with earbuds by a brand new headstone,
a hammer-knife parked nearby, the driver smoking a J

Mesh

What was going through your mind in the rose garden
that afternoon we lay under the bushes, in chopped sunlight that
        checkered our bodies
        and your bare legs, the roses blighted with the first frost,
you touching my face, cigarette unlit, nobody but us?
        Left later that day to visit Morristown—

business section in the back seat of a Ford Galaxy I would later wreck,
        cigarette smoke coming out the driver's window

—but it is as if you just left me
because there's this girl sitting at a table in the courtyard by the
        Princeton library.
        She's wearing mesh and sipping a Swiss Miss—
        how I wish you could see this—
                —and it's thirty out, and windy,
and the reticulated light and shadow checkerboards her long bare
        legs

but she just reads on, the sun in each lens of her shades, with her
        love, I guess,
        to keep her warm,
and me with this thought of you, how only you
        would wear mesh on a day like this.

J. T. Barbarese

Postulates

Aesthetics: the study
of what is sensuous
and useless.

I made bad confessions,
then bad communions,
just to follow you home.

*

God made the rational numbers,
all the rest
are human inventions.

Ah, all those
torn-out centerfolds
I sailed over your fence.

*

God and the imagination
are one,
but do not get along.

While you knelt to receive,
on my knees, way in back,
I caressed you.

*

Time is a man,
Blake said,
Space is a woman.

The Peano postulates
are incomplete. So what.
So are we.

Creed

I emptied the poor box and fed the nickels and dimes to a meter, a
    gumball dispenser, a slot,
I brought the leaded glass to an antique shop on South, and the
    pews became bonfires and block parties
with chicken dinners from the kosher butchers on the other side of
    Broad, everything set on the altar for the vets
who spend Sunday morning detoxing, chain smoking on somebody's
    front step, getting chased off,
damning their sons sonofabitching their daughters so stupefied by
    compulsory education compulsory religion compulsory
    marriage,
and missing their grandmothers, who were still taking the trolley to
    the garment factory every morning, age 67, on partial SSI,
coming home to her own row house, working miracle Campbell
    Soup dinners for two, getting weekend meats from Nunzio
    the Chicken Man on Point Breeze,
cursing whatever God kills a husband and leaves a woman a widow
    at 30 with six children a mortgage and no insurance,
married to a 32nd degree Mason who translated for Pershing, the
    only insurance salesman in history to die uninsured,
leaving me alone so I could read *Les mariés de la tour Eiffel* stolen
    from Temple's library in that back room with a window and
    a record player and a French dictionary,
or walk up to the University Museum, four miles each way, and to
    walk back happy,
letting me have my privacy, letting me work late into sometimes
    summer mornings,
or sleep late on Saturdays and Sundays with no bother about
    obligations,
or sleep even later that morning in June after the assassination in the
    hotel kitchen after the California primary

leaving me to mourn alone under the railroad bridge 25th and
      Washington, leaving me just a note,
Coffee on the range just turn on the gas love you Gran.

Vinyl

The summer I bought *Pet Sounds* at G.C. Murphy's, I hadn't gone a
    block from the store when on impulse I shattered the album
against a lamp post in Girard Park between the make-out benches
    and the box wood bushes.
I was out three dollars but felt weirdly relieved—of war terror,
    Johnson terror, ICBM terror—and shook the bourgeois
    sleeve just to hear the vinyl rattle.
A year later, I was stopped by a homeless vet in Chicago
inside the Greyhound station. Buzzed, he mistook me for one of
    three Army buddies killed in one of our wars,
and number three looked like me (he said), so I gave him my
    panhandled cash and felt the same relief—no home-keeping
    youth now, no witless boy—
but broke, now, I thumbed two rides eight-hundred miles, hearing
    the continuing news about the *Pueblo* and the old news
    about Otis Redding,
and thought about Rachel Wagner, who sang me "God Only knows"
    through an electrified pig fence
before kissing me in cold Boscobel, while her mother did the dishes
    and her father milked cows, our strange breaths twinned,
    then conjoint, thought of her
singing "If you should ever leave me, / life would go on, believe me,"
all truck-ride long, the pig corn in my jacket clucking and baby-
    rattling, which was when my thought turned again to that
    vinyl
as the ravens settled on fences and the breaths of the Ohio cows
did pliés over their muzzles. *Who needs vinyl!* I said to the guy at the
    wheel, who had no idea,
because I was ecstatic at last, relieved of the memory of crumbled
    vinyl and shattered rock 'n' roll,

of how a panhandled dollar looks good in an empty hand,
how the music came back a thousandfold while the pigs looked on.

J. T. Barbarese

Haloes

Above the canal banks
scoured
by a week's

horizontal rain
a hawk circles
(over beached crates and treed rags,

an inverted kayak, soccer balls and beer cans)
and echoes
the opalescent

haloes in the half-thawed
D&R below,
beside me—

I call it my hawk, each one of its orbits
the octave of a turtle's
hitting the surface

when spooked by
passersby —
still hibernation-doped

and half-asleep the turtles
scram from the fallen limbs
where they park, necks tilted

to warm their beaks
and sun their shells,
until I come

crunching the gravel
and they peel off
in sloppy twos and threes,

hit the half-thawed surface
and make these holes
that refreeze, nightly,

into aureoles
haloes
crimped crowns

all knock-offs of the hawk's
wiry
circles in the air—

paired flights,
one fled, one flying,
and a third

thing too—
a means that works
its ends

while nothing attends,
the turtles gone back
into native mud,

my hawk gone wherever,
these footprints
in a frozen stew—

clay, leaf-fall, gravel, goose droppings—
as night comes on
and ices whatever moves.

The Night He Picked Up Wallace Stevens

in his cab, the stars were out
and danced on the windshield, Stevens wrote,
in his poem about my father.

They danced like skaters on the slick glass
and in their reel and tinseling, he saw
the whole of life as a taxi ride through Philadelphia.

Not reading poetry, not recognizing his passenger,
those were the years he might have picked up Frost,
Eliot, even Pound, who grew up in Wyncote,

but the only fare he knew on sight was John Carradine
who he insisted was Italian
because his last name ended in a vowel.

If you did not look too close, Pop said,
stars looked better in the rear view.
So did he. In the poem about him

he wonders when his life will come to something,
if it's all been worth it. The wife,
the three boys, that one huge financial reversal …

so he taxis stars in a yellow cab, and
his meter runs, and the motor runs
and his time runs out.

The Dead House

Fireplace blocked,
sealed with
cardboard, and taped.
Furniture trashed,
paneling smashed.
On the second floor

mid-corridor,
a rotting cat
furry and fey
in a nap
of gore
glued flat

to a spot
on the floor,
ether-sweet
in a frieze of decay,
up-staring, pop-eyed,
pissed.

The screens I installed
belled out, belled in.
Every window
cracked, broken,
or forgotten, left open.
The in-gusting Atlantic
left smelling sick.

A shade softly crashed
on a sash,
finish-nails and a bare
molly-bolt fan-fared
me from the gloom.

Google the address:
from outer space
it's a bare green blot,
treeless, erased,
terns where we made love,
gulls where we fought.

J. T. Barbarese

Reading Primo Levi off Columbus Circle

Re-reading him in Bouchon
past noon, midtown mobbed,
like an ant-farm seen through painkillers.
God, what a bust it's all been,

capitalism, communism, feminism,
this lust to liberate.
Ché should have stayed in medicine.
The women here say they can't wait

to marry to get to the alimony
before they hit thirty. The men,
heads skinned like *Lager* inmates,
know only the revolutions

in diets and spinning classes.
And yet, one table away,
these two, with gnarled, empretzeled hands,
seem unhappy in the old way.

Silver Alert

The lanyard over the knob traced
a widow's walk in space.
The roads are filled with old folk on the loose.

Once they were babes gumming binkies,
with monkeys with cymbals and trolls on the shag,
while giants with bible-paper skin bent down
and smiled guillotines,
and wide-eyed they googled back,
edible as pies.

O elders, twisting Kleenex into folds
for Frosted Curls in her gym shoes,
                on the road all alone,
grieve for all who go missing,
and wander where we all wander,
our license plate known,
our place unknown.
The babes' eyes will dry into black thumbtacks
and their smiles thin into equators
and they too will lean over breakfast maps
and ponder 11 down, 14 across.

Rumor Has It

"Twelve years running. Always in the spring,
Abe would lead Ike hogtied up the hill
A day before the boy's birthday. He'd open his bible,
Find the page, pile kindling, then start swinging
This beat-up old butcher's blade (Sarah's,
Come down her family). He'd swing it over his head
With Ike scared and cuffed to a bed of green wood—
And not a goddamn thing would happen. Every year
Twelve years running.
                              Ike turned out ok,
Given all that. Though most of us did understood
You don't go wishing young Ike a happy birthday.
Anyway, day he turns thirteen, he leaves for good.
When the old man died, Sarah embraced the Lord Jesus.
Last I heard Ike went off and joined the circus."

Obit

"'An imagined place where a rope-ladder bridge, hid
beneath trailing willows, sags under pursuers—
rebel guardian angels—who have paused mid-
stride and plan to smuggle you out of bed later,
after the rides have closed! The sun is the donkey's
ass, clouds pinned-on, and Luna the pinner's
palm …" Was this his vision of reality,
God throwing a pizza party?"
                              Sort of. And prayer
a thirtyish mom hanging clothes some morning in April,
singing *Mein Herr Bis du Schein* to her firstborn.
He celebrated ambivalence, the transformations
of mess into magic, and especially how the Fallen Angels
shouted back at God, 'You created the oyster.
No big deal. The oyster created the pearl.'"

J. T. Barbarese

"One of the Many"

—and nine, or not even,
all dolled up in her mismatched best—
scarification, paint, shell beads,
a Gap tee over a sari —
dragged down a dirt road,
hamstrung, raped, shot.
One of the many
they limed
till her color rhymed
with the zombie-white petals
from the apple blossoms
that fall on my *Geographic*'s
waxed fold-out this morning.
White as the cherry blossoms,
white as what ate her face
and effaced her,
white on the scrim of her sleep.

Red Light Rapture

Quitting time
    & out of the clutter
into the foot-traffic,
    I am gathered in,
& stand rapt
    & behold the gutter.
Bubbles igloo to
    the top
as does whatever seeks light,
    rich detritus,
a penny and two dimes,
    gravel and asphalt
and a spent match skateboarding
    into the sewer
where the gutter dispatches
    pedestrian visions
once the light turns green,
    and I cross the street—
mind in the gutter,
5 p.m., 15th and Vine.

Listening to a Book while Driving

Leaves on the windshield, gravel under my tires,
geese overhead 7 a.m.
listening to the last book you bought me
remembering the smell of my truck's cab,
the sudden shocked stink of the gingkoes
near the Amish meeting,
the Etch-a-Sketch starling murmurations after work, driving home,
        near sunset,

me thinking *What a life* me saying *Christ am I lucky*

should have been wiser,
mindful of death driving over the leaves, of savagery
in the starlings, hardly playthings, like fistfuls of stones thrown at
        the sun,
of the tipped uterus, the abortion, isoniazid and TB and
        Legionnaire's,
the Sinais of junked cars becoming Everests, trucks burned to their
        axles, compacts recompacted and pancaked thin as foil,
the stench of the homeless, the sick smell of their need,
the dead skunk smell of hash coming from that middle school back
        there in my rear-view, the crossing guard looking the wrong
        way, waving STOP

skeptical of sweet plaster hallways and your hair under my palm,
of snow-covered leaves like white three-fingered Mickey Mouse
        gloves,
and of these lights, green as the thousands of days behind me.

A Lonely Woman in a Coffee Shop

DNA and the I Ch'ing
                won't sort out loneliness,
straighten your hair, level luck's
                uneven fields.
Bliss is mostly chemical.

But your wire-rims cast perfect circles
                on your worthless book,
your corn-rows gleam
                and limn your sunken cheeks,
and the moon's chin
                (sort of like yours)
nearly touches its nose
                over the statue of Billy Penn.

So, join me.
        I'll save you a place,
we'll be lonely together. Good coffee,
        bright sun for companions,
one mug to a window.

Halloween

Every store on Chestnut
blinks a moon- or flashlit face,
and the loser on the vent
at Walnut grins a picket
fence when a sudden taxi
torches him. Homely in repose
and semi-lotus squat, he knows
what's what because he either sees
or wears it. A handful of punks
from the Northeast, pure trash,
come pouring from the subway—
piratical, pierced, mohawked, eye-patched—
and one points a stickbat
at this unsexed lump then
hawks a greenie into the cap
and they scatter onto Locust.
Hulk and Hellboy show up
and stare at the Jeff cap
and its filthy small fortune,
as I add my dumb change
and say nothing, half-
distracted by three leggy
twenty-something drunks
in Pipi Longstocking duds
blacked teeth rose-blotted cheeks
licking fake chocolate cones
and spinning their pigtails at me.
The light balloons overhead
and the darkness sucks it
down and coughs up silhouettes
of City Hall and Billy Penn

marching into the dark. The wreck
on the vent has enough for his pint,
but who am I to begrudge or judge
him or his stubborn comfort? His
is the perfect homelessness
—uncompromised, unmasked,
Lear's bare forked animal
made up as what he is—man unmade,
the *what* that inhabits the *who*
when the civilized habits go,
half-lit on his cold vent tonight
while the children of light greet
the children of the dark
in the middle of Broad Street.

J.T. Barbarese

Waking to Total Uselessness

Deer crossed the woods —
    five deer,
a tight dignified family—
covered with fog.
I wondered what I had done all my life
    as they stepped into the fog
safe from my uselessness,
    which is dangerous.
They passed nobly and regally
a slow tango
past the dialysis clinics, post offices, and dollar stores,
    out of sight of the druggist,
the guy on the cherry-picker over the highway,
    him on the hammer-knife mowing the park
below the stalled high-rise, the liquor mart, the cop
    aiming a hair-dryer (radar gun) into the fog,
beyond the rotting road-beds, the still-life with front-end loader
and sixty-inch sewer main,
past the befogged meadow where they pause
    statuesque, sleepy, poised,
beyond smudge pot, toolshed, jackhammer, baled chicken wire,
snapped trees and the wind-feathered,
flattened, flyaway crime tape
long and yellow and ratty.
When they vanished
at the tree line,
something gripped me
as the sun lit my unmade bed,
the command center of my uselessness,
and began climbing the walls.

Useless to turn away, nothing to do
    except commemorate

how it slowly candled the maples
did the sky up like a clown
dolled up the fog,
    and in minutes solved the world
into a unified expression of what never varies—
paired ducks on the river below,
the goshawk that lives on the roof
circling the river—
with or without me.

There and Not There

A mediation on the question *was it all worth it*
his memoir recounts his

finding himself suddenly "coming to"
as if from a coma

in the middle of a banquet
and the recognition

that age had advanced on him glacially.
Then the gash down the plane of the east

by an abrupting left-handed mountain
not there yesterday

(called Mount Was,
ecclesiastically white,

a master's watercolor of novena candles)
shocked him like the smell of shoe polish and blood

the day of the May procession when they sang
Queen of the angels queen of the May

(lyric by J.H. Newman?) to the young Mary Pat Sweeney
whose father worked for the FBI

and whose morals entered a fascinating decline
after she left the convent, then college, then two marriages,

for runways in Paris, TX; Athens, GA; Troy, NY; and Smyrna, DE.
His answer is *probably not*

because he can't put up with or away
the sight of this mountain
blocking his self-view.

J. T. Barbarese

En Route

*Whether in fiction or reality, most Romantic poets eventually turned into
bourgeois capitalists.*
—Graham Robb, *Rimbaud*

All over wherever we are the waves are making
eyes at me as if having some sort of vision.
The waves tsk-tsk against the hull.
The deck rocks like an imbecile,
the stacks are davenning and half-visible
whales with cowlicks spout the way.
The playfulness of the postmodern has
a vitality that somehow makes my emptiness
          a prerequisite to its fullness—I could even say
this feels like a rehearsal of the Seven Days.
          The breakers pun on the gulls, the gulls on eyes,
eyes on distant arches, which is why
nothing is ever one thing, and why
when and if
I get wherever I am going –my
destiny beckons like the tower on the cover
of an alumni brochure—
I'll rethink everything,
join the smelly mob with its static present
and combination second-person-singular-plural,
abandon the subjunctive and grow
unforgettable by teaming with the unspeakable.
I will be done with history and become the glare
off the radiant emptiness out there.

Poussiniana

for Christine Walden

Twenty-four panes to the window,
a hand of water rolling on its axis,
and waterfowl on Burnham Pond, preening.
He lifts the saw to the wounded limb.
Moss on the oak, leaves on the lawn.
The angelsbreath bowing the air,
the cat watching a bee
bang against the glass.
There's this, there's that.

There is so much here to remember
you forget the waxing Sunday afternoon
or the geraniums growing beside you.
You forget that there are deep sumps in the far hills,
the overlaid tornado tracks,
or Carrie Foster, who owns the woods,
who dresses like a man and who lives alone.
You forget about Tempe Wicke, who hid her horse
in her bedroom from the rebels—
all this, all that.

The present is just this once,
the limb is meeting the ground,
you can hear the earthworm
heaving
in the garden.

J. T. Barbarese

Cartouche

Hurray for what comes
from desire.
It alone

survives, the rest
is the lecture.
Hurray to the sun

on the glass. Watch
it kiss
whatever is—shoe-top to

bald infant head—
on its quiet campaign.
Joy parties

hard by day
while our dust just gathers.
That black shape

traced on the ground
at noon
is you minus yours.

Children's Hour

On the saloon's flat-screen:
in-screen of Tebow tebowing
over a sacked museum,
a stubbed-out factory stack,
pairs of shredded boots,
dead kids. Slow pan
to a muscular Christian
with burning eyes, Metallica tats,
one-percent body fat
and a bouncer's tan.

We suck bones, sip beer.
We lack the vision of evil,
reflect on our complicity
while a heat-seeking SSM
swims off to eat a bridge.
What's cooking, I wonder,
in those puffy body bags?
The God that does not exist
comes with lots of baggage.

Invisible Methodists
sing *Penniless, we own the world*
as Cheltenham High's Bibi the Bully,
all grown up, in moody pinstripes,
holds a pointer. History wants an affair,
not a relationship,
but moves in anyway.

A dissolve to close-ups of the displaced,
nobodies who look up at somebodies,

at us guiltless things surprised
who ride the Dow-Jones crawl,
timeshares among timeservers,
not minding the difference.

Scatter

I was reading Finley
in a Settlement waiting room
secure in my obscurity

when I heard him down the corridor
playing his scales
before we ran out of money

and he gave up the piano.
History is perfected
in the person and the person

is a scatter.
A girl with a red cat
and prayer wheel of daily meds,

a man winding a motor on the table
over a Lucky and coffee,
a girl with plaster horses

in some mansion,
Für Elise from a balcony,
sunny and empty,

or that boy on that bike,
wind at his back,
jacket ballooning.

J. T. Barbarese

Cancer

Denise Gess (1952–2009)

Death is your pilot
flying your body
back to its long home,

the body's a banquet
and the soul
comes clean off the bone,

and the soul is a wolf
driven by winter
to feed on air.

Conditional Compassion

The light has the glister of guano that glistens in caves,
and the roses are dying in their beds, one by one, as they should.
They know their time is come. So many of these
kids, in fall regalia. Their sincerity is deafening.

Calamity gives me the munchies—bombings in housing projects,
evil like random numbers encrypting whole countries,
only women and children left, all the men gone to die,
babes in arms, babushkas staring down empty tracks.

Chaos has its own color scheme. The land breaks out
in yellowing steeples, graying, Stonhenges of rubble.
Here a lynched sneaker, there an arm, flies on the knuckles,
encorpsed Bacon canvasses, flesh stuck to fenders,
methane-inflated humps, party yellow, Bukowski's favorite color …
No moms yelling at kids, no village idiot
picking his teeth with a stickmatch. Just

the heart's putt-putt, the beat of Absolute Geist,
the cows drifting like empty frigates
over Farmer Brown's north forty, all tails and concentration,
for the soul has gone Novembering with Jaco and Glenn Gould,
                Lawrence and Emily and Oscar.
The moon has rammed a cloud. The sun milks shade,
late apples on the table. They apple with joy,
appling diaphanously, about ready to bleed.

Fruit Basket Covered with Cloth

by the truck stop on the way to the house of the old friend, an old
      man now, with the setters,
for the smartly dressed woman who came up the aisle telling us
      to turn off our phones and direct all comments to the
      ventriloquist and not the dummy,
by Walt, who woke in the morning and thought God had left it as a
      house gift after a sleep-over,
where the two roads meet near Colossus, at the crossing of the
      imperiled and the imperishable, where Edgar kills Edmund,
in the rain glimpsed from the streaked cab of a van stopped at a
      light,
on the arm of a candy-striper in her late teens, getting on or off an
      elevator and smelling of cigarettes,
in the wind, on a round metal table, central rocking umbrella, gray
      concrete slab,
seashore, day, laughing gulls, bright lotion, shouts of joy, scent of
      surf, sound of surf-thunder,
in shadow, as if a landscape, cool white cloth codpiece, the off-in-
      the-corner figure, considering quitting, for the day or for
      good, the thing in front of him seeming
mediocre and sloppy and not startled and a little tentative, as art
      should be,
upended, the cloth underneath, one newly picked peach, crushed,
filled with snow and window weights on the porch of a rancher
      (second owner), Rockport, IL, pickup in the driveway, no
      hood, gravity-fed gas tank,
stuffed with peeps, plastic grass, chocolate eggs and tiny cards with
      names in light pencil,
tail-wagging dog looking on,

in the vestibule of the house of the aunt who waits in her bedroom
       for her nephew, twenty and a virgin, who picks the note off
       the cloth *Shower first I put out towels*
and in the mind of the grown man who saves it then loses it over a
       life's moves and cities and states
and still knows it by heart

staring out at a road crew raking gravel out of a dump truck, the
       gravel white and heaped and bulging.

J. T. Barbarese

Lullaby

for Julianna

What little hisses the grass makes, and not a lot now.
The slightly Japanese tint to the sky is yours,
and so is the tilt of the sky, and the building clouds,
and the birds peeled from their shadows as they take off.
The clouds are wind's short lyrics, then there's the smoke
stiff as shriveled necks, the factory stacks
I can't think of a name for. You're there all along

postponing night for a while. The twilight is stoked
with purple—the clouds are holding a prom.
The west won't quite get dark. It is a cloth
for the wine-stain sun, the east is tunneled out
for the rockabye moon. There is far too much there.
Things coalesce from their brokenness. Night
is their convalescence. It has no edges.

The stars in the water study you, the fireworks too,
the bristling and thorned things. The winds love you
so the weeds sing. So does the air,
the freckled spots on the leaves,
the rusted hinges, the dust as it fills
the sunlight, the sunbeams like straws sucking the pooled rains.

It is all really nothing and it cannot last,
so be alive now. You once were not here.
You are here now. I pretend you were always here.

Instructions

This is for teaching verse.
This is for teaching rhyme.
This, for meter.
Carriage means hearse,
Juliet, tomb,
The Rock is Peter.

This is for pity,
This is for mercy,
Love is relentless.
It's raining on Cutie,
And rain equals death.
Translation, resistance.

Here, love laps the lovers.
There, it flags at the finish.
A twat is a cowl.
Here, there is no there.
The past knew many grandmothers.
Then equals now.

Here, love dies in an email,
The unspeakable is spoken
And him equals her.
The sun warms the blind,
The cider jug swallows the rain.
Smoke in her hair.

J. T. Barbarese

In the end, love is betrayal,
Beauty avoids your eyes,
Passion is barter.
They look and still find nothing.
Tell them to look in their hearts.
Tell them to look harder.

Agnostic Kaddish

Adios smoke, dust, honeybee, sunbeam,
adios carpet tack, lily, fry pan, hod, hood and handhold
bona fortuna lunar eclipse, tuna fish, peach blossom, dog shit,
      maggot and garbage can,
   thought and non-thought,
auf wiedersehen wrought iron gate, stained glass transom, iron lawn
      wicket, molly bolt, sundial,
nomina patris et filii et spiritus sancti super omnes omniaque sunt
goodbye all, goodbye all of it,

goodbye spring water, gravy boat, crystal decanters, compotes,
goodbye wine, beer, vodka, brandy, mimosa, cosmopolitan,
goodbye (while I think of it) cosmos,
goodbye staple, pocket litter, nail paring, bird feather, body fluff,
      penny, pubic hair, seeded bagel, crumb cake and cookie,
goodbye mic stand, sycamore bark-sheddings, clothespin and
      clothesline and clothes prop,
goodbye carpets, carpet tacks, carpet glue, carpet mold, carport and
      carry-ons,
goodbye plugs, adapters, IC boards, solder and hot glue, staple gun,
      router, chop saw, finish plane, roughing plane, jigsaw and
      saw blade,
goodbye tree mold, linseed and turpentine and varnish
      spontaneously combusting in the far room where the baby
      slept
*

bye bye ring of mystery keys to forty lost locations,
bye bye secret key that unlocked a jewelry box,
bye bye key to the shed at the shore house, bye bye shore house,
bye bye key to the filing cabinet, bye bye filing cabinet,

bye bye apartment key, bye bye borrowed and never returned key to
    the Myers house,
bye bye key to Andrew's Cadillac, Andrew dead, Caddy totaled,
bye bye all they unlocked, all they locked and locked up,
bye bye key to the front door and key to the back door and key to
    my first car,
bye bye front door, back door, cellar door, house, porch, porch glider,
bye bye car, stuff in the trunk, tire iron, wheel chock, inflatable
    mattress,
bye bye box of mother-in-law's human ashes, bye bye gray duct tape
    and ashen spare,
bye bye jump cables, farewell extra battery, foldout chair, sand bucket
    and spade,
farewell fungo, bat donuts, batting gloves, left-handed catcher's mitt,
    first aid kit,
bye bye Mt Airy, bye bye Ventnor, bye bye Girard Park, bye bye FDR
    Park, bye bye East and West River Drives, bye bye BQE,
bye bye north south east west, working week and day of rest,
so long directions, panel trucks, street signs, sky writers, bye bye sky,
sun moon stars etcetera bye bye bye

*

bye bye Ernie Ball Slinky 10s, bye bye stubby plectrum, bye bye
    ratty gig bag,
bye bye brushes transistors gas can funnel,
bye bye punctuation grammar syntax typology the six declensions of
    εννεπειν,
bye bye Liddel and Scott, *Tutti I Verbi Greci*
bye bye gold wedding rings, bye bye old wristwatch,
bye bye pirate bank, bye bye acetylene torch, pipe dope els pipe caps
    solder wire

bye by primaries, especially beloved green and blue, aquamarine, all
 except black,
bye bye cigars and old door knobs and underground bicycle bells,
 for a while anyway,
ta ta to acorns, acorns, acorns, so many spring acorns, summer green
 so green it saddens me,
bye bluebirds, dogs, squirrels, fox, deer, geese, hawks, egrets and
 turtles
(just waking up now, warm sunshine alarm clock)
bye analog clocks, bye digital clocks, bye clock on the Camden
 Municipal Services building,
bye bye Dean and Deluca's, Amil DeLucia the luthier, Ninth Street
 and Giordano's,
be bye Sly, bye bye Fitzie, bye bye Llama, bye bye Joe, bye bye Billy,
 bye bye Kenn,
bye bye angry wounds, bye bye hernias, bye bye dental pain, bye bye
 dizziness and vertigo (also the movie), good riddance lower
 back,
bad right eye, bad left ear, torn right rotor, so many scars
bye bye Lynch, Hitchcock, Scorsese, Disney's *Pinocchio,*
bye bye man on the shoulder changing his tire, girl pulled over
 by statie, young man on his cell obeying the law, looking
 stressed and unsmiling,
bye bye distinct and vague recollections, bye bye dark large eyes and
 abandoned airs, bye bye culinary geniuses,
bye bye one-on-one at Vare under midnight lights, bye bye shagging
 fly balls,
bye bye roadkill, bye bye kill corridor on 295 South, bye bye
 Mishamobile, bye bye Yaris and Ford Explorer, Dodge with
 pushbutton trans, and a special so long to Christine's Ford
 Galaxie with that huge mill, car I totaled,

bye bye Christine first love bye bye Loren Eisely, bye bye Allen's
    Books,
bye conspiracy theories, JFK, MLK, all of them except the one
    about Jesus,

*

Bouchon, bye bye, soft pretzel, yoga mat, mustard, vendor, roast
    chestnut smoke,
Bye girl stink boy stink butt stink smell of human body, pampers in
    trash cans,
Bye gym shorts, white socks, overalls, Cat In The Hat pjs, dragon
    slippers, Japanese scarves,
Bye lovely Asian lady in long black coat, my god what white skin,
Bye whiteness and poached eggs, coffee and dry rye toast,
Bye croissants, apple fritters, dead rat at Broadway and 52nd,
Bye handsome Italian man and the beautiful way he said *Balducci's,*
And the way Rebecca pronounced the Spanish in *Blood Meridian,*
    the way she said *Abuelita, digame,* and the way it made me
    grin,

Am I not like Apollinaire, I never expected leave-taking without the
    leaving, but there it is,
I never expected to hear the woman outside the monument turn and
    say *Si, di Roma, son',*
or be thinking about it now,
Or see her pirouetting up to her man, touching a finger to his lips,

And I never expected the lily, the seagulls in the parlor, terns in the
    sweater drawer, starlings in the coffee,
The tuna salad embronzed, or the crazy doctor's kiss, how she took
    my hand,

Or the tiny round tables, pink pants, my old suede jacket,
Or the Shunk Street library, the library of Alexandria, all the
       libraries *et cetera*
Or the windows filled with leather pants sunshine and boots,
Windows broken and decorated for Easter, bow windows and
       basement and casement, and the falling glass,
Or to have to ask where to stop, or yet another translation of Dante,
       or the German editions of *Mad,* or Chinese microwave
       instructions,
Or never see some again while they were alive,
Or to have read all of Austen and Mailer and Delillo and Pound,
Or to think of security guards and gutters, hardwood floors and
       violets and young girls with their hair wrapped in towels
       when I hear certain names.

ACKNOWLEDGMENTS

Boulevard: "Cartouche," "Lullaby," "Instructions," "Children's Hour," "Cancer," and "Conditional Compassion."

The Denver Quarterly: "Red Light Rapture."

The Hopkins Review: "Creed."

Measure: "Rumor Has It."

Pearl: "One of the Many."

Plume: "En Route," "Halloween," and "No Selfies for Mary."

Poetry: "Reading Primo Levi off Columbus Circle," "The Dead House."

The New Criterion: "On a Sentence from Benjamin" and "Scatter."

The New Yorker: "There and Not There" and "The Night He Picked Up Wallace Stevens."

The Sewanee Review: "A Lonely Woman in a Coffee Shop" and "Waking to Total Uselessness."

Sub-Tropics: "Haloes."

"Poussiniana" appeared in *Visiting Wallace: Poems Inspired by the Life and Work of Wallace Stevens,* ed. Dennis Barone and James Finnegan (University of Iowa Press, 2009).

ABOUT THE AUTHOR

True Does Nothing is **J.T. BARBARESE**'s sixth collection of poems. His poems and translations have appeared in the *Atlantic Monthly, Boulevard, Poetry, The New Yorker,* and *The Times Literary Supplement.* He has also published fiction in *Boulevard* and *Narrative,* and essays, reviews and literary journalism in *Poetry, The Georgia Review, Threepenny Review,* and the *Wall Street Journal.* He teaches literature and creative writing at Rutgers University in Camden, New Jersey.

www.ingramcontent.com/pod-product-compliance
Lightning Source LLC
Chambersburg PA
CBHW022153090426
42742CB00010B/1499